Stage 2
Longman
Structural
Readers

Foul Play

L. G. Alexander
Illustrated
by Tim Howe

Part 1: The new neighbour

Hawkins' General Store is the only shop in the small village of Puddleton. On Saturday, the shop was full of people. They were buying things and, of course, they were talking!

Mrs Carpe was very excited. "Have you heard the news?" she asked her friend, Mrs Plunkett.

"News? What news?" Mrs Plunkett asked.

Mrs Carpe whispered the secret into Mrs Plunkett's ear.

"No? Really?" Mrs Plunkett cried. She was very excited. "Have you heard the news?"

All the people in the shop were very excited.

"What news?" they cried.

"It's a secret," she whispered.

"Tell us! Tell us!" they all shouted. "Tell us the secret!"

Mrs Carpe pushed in front of Mrs Plunkett. "It's *my* secret," she said. "*I'm* going to tell you." She was very excited.

The shop was very quiet.

"Angus MacFee has got a new neighbour!" Mrs Carpe said.

"A new neighbour?" Mrs Nosey Parker cried. "What's this neighbour's name?"

"Plumley. Mrs Maisie Plumley. She's a widow."

Mrs Carpe smiled. "She's from the city. She has never lived in a village."

"Mm," Mrs Nosey said. "A city woman, eh? She's just come to Puddleton! She's a widow and Angus is a widower!"

3

Mrs Maisie Plumley is a large and happy woman. She is very busy today. She has to clean her house. She has to put things in their place. She has to cook a nice meal. She's a very good cook!

I've got to do a lot of work in this house and a lot of work in the garden, she thought, but it doesn't matter. Life is so good here. Life is so quiet in this beautiful village! The air is so clean. She smiled happily.

Then she went into the garden.
   Mm. I'll have to do a lot of work in this garden. Life here will be very nice. I can hear the birds in the trees. I can smell the flowers in the fields.

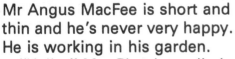

Mr Angus MacFee is short and thin and he's never very happy. He is working in his garden.

"Hello," Mrs Plumley called. "I'm your new neighbour. My name is Maisie Plumley."

"Hello," Angus said.

"I'm Angus MacFee. How do you do? Is your husband at home?"

"I'm a widow," Maisie said.

"I'm a widower," Angus said.

"Oh, I'm sorry," Maisie said. She smiled and he smiled, too.

"This is Henry," Angus said. "He's my best friend."

"He's a very fine rooster," Maisie said, and the rooster crowed: *Cock-a-doodle-doo!*

"Too late, Henry," Angus said. "It's ten o'clock in the morning!"

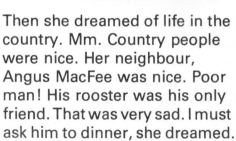

Part 2: Cock-a-doodle-doo!

Maisie Plumley went to bed early. It was her first night in Puddleton. It was a fine night, so she opened the window.

Ah! Nice clean air, she thought. A beautiful night!

Maisie Plumley dreamed of life in the city. Ugh! She didn't like life in the city. The air was dirty. There were a lot of cars. There were a lot of people. There was a lot of noise. The city was a bad place.

Then she dreamed of life in the country. Mm. Country people were nice. Her neighbour, Angus MacFee was nice. Poor man! His rooster was his only friend. That was very sad. I must ask him to dinner, she dreamed.

6

Suddenly, in her sleep, Maisie heard a loud noise: once, then again. She woke up and looked at her watch. It was 3 a.m. She sat up in bed and heard the noise again: *Cock-a-doodle-doo!*

Oh, it's Henry, she thought.

The next night, Maisie woke up again. She looked at her watch. It was 2 a.m. Henry crowed again very loudly. He crowed all night. *Cock-a-doodle-doo!*

Poor Maisie! She tried to sleep, but she couldn't!

The next night, Maisie woke up again. She looked at her watch. It was 1 a.m. Henry crowed loudly. *Cock-a-doodle-doo! Cock-a-doodle-doo!*

That silly rooster, she thought. He never knows the time.

7

The next day, Maisie Plumley met Mrs Carpe in the street.

"How are you? How's life in our village?" Mrs Carpe asked.

"Oh, it's very nice. I love the village. I love the country. I love my new house, but . . ."

"But what?" Mrs Carpe asked.

"Well, I wake up a lot."

"Oh," Mrs Carpe laughed. "Angus MacFee's rooster wakes you up. He's a silly bird. He never knows the time and he wakes up the village."

"But it's worse for *me*," Maisie said. "I live next door."

"Yes," Mrs Carpe said. "You must speak to Angus."

"I can't," Maisie said. "What can I say to him? That rooster is his only friend."

The women in Hawkins' General Store listened to the sad story.

"Maisie Plumley likes our village, but she wakes up a lot," said Mrs Carpe.

"She dreams of Angus, so she wakes up," Mrs Nosey said.

"No," Mrs Carpe answered. "She wakes up because that silly rooster crows all night. Listen!"

Cock-a-doodle-doo!

"See? It's crowing now and it's eleven o'clock. That bird can't tell day from night."

"We must help Maisie Plumley," Mrs Plunkett said. "She's a good woman, but what can we do? We can't speak to Angus. Poor man! That silly rooster is his only friend. It's his only friend in the world!"

9

  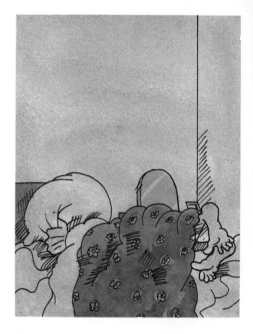

It was a fine warm night but Maisie shut the window.

I must stop the noise, she thought.

But she couldn't. At 3 a.m. she heard *Cock-a-doodle-doo!* Henry crowed very loudly.

The next night, Maisie shut the window and put wax in her ears.

But at 2 a.m. Henry crowed louder than before: *Cock-a-doodle-doo!* The wax didn't stop the noise.

The next night, Maisie shut the window, put wax in her ears and put a big towel over her head. She put her head under her pillow and pulled the pillow over her ears, but Henry crowed all night and she didn't sleep.

A month later, Maisie Plumley wasn't a happy woman. She was always tired. She didn't cook nice meals. She didn't go into the garden. She didn't listen to the birds in the trees.

She sat in her kitchen and tried to sleep – but she couldn't. *Cock-a-doodle-doo!*

He crows all day and he crows all night. He never sleeps, she thought. What can I do? Oh, what can I do?

Perhaps the city isn't so bad, she thought. She was tired, but she was angry, too, very angry.

That silly bird can't do this to me, she thought. I won't speak to Angus. *He* can't stop his bird, but perhaps *I* can!

Part 3: Murder!
It's Saturday night. It's 1 a.m. and it's very dark. There aren't any stars in the sky. There are only big black clouds. It's cold and windy. Two black cats are sitting on Maisie's garden wall.

There aren't any lights in the windows of the houses in Puddleton. There aren't any lights in Maisie's windows. Angus MacFee's windows are dark, too. Angus is sleeping and Henry is sleeping, too!

But there's a figure in the dark. The figure is in Angus's garden. The figure is wearing a black coat and is walking quietly to the shed in the garden. Look! What is in the figure's hand?

Yes, we can see it now! It's an axe. The figure is pushing the door of the shed. The door makes a noise, so the figure stops. Then the figure opens the door wider and goes into the shed.

Now the figure has switched on a torch. What can we see in the light of the torch? Look! We can see Henry. Henry isn't sleeping now. He has opened one eye and he is looking at the figure in the shed.

Henry thinks: It's morning! Look at his neck! He is going to crow and wake up the village with a loud *Cock-a-doodle-doo!*

The figure is holding the axe and is looking at Henry's neck, too!

Suddenly, the figure jumps and takes Henry by the neck!

What's happening? Henry doesn't understand. He is trying to crow, but he can't. There is a hand round his neck. Henry's tongue is going up and down!

Crash! The axe has come down on Henry's neck! Poor Henry! He has lost his head and he will never crow again. Now the figure is putting Henry into a big black bag. That's the end of Henry!

Now the figure has switched off the torch and has opened the shed door. The door makes a noise again. The figure waits in the dark and then pushes the door and goes quietly into Angus MacFee's garden.

Angus is dreaming. He is dreaming of happier days. But in his sleep he can hear the door of his shed. It is making a lot of noise. Angus turns in his sleep. He is now dreaming of Henry in the shed and he is smiling.

The two black cats have come off the wall and are now in Angus's garden. They're making a loud noise in the night. They are crying like babies. The figure looks at the cats and stands quietly in the garden.

Angus turns in his sleep again and then suddenly wakes up. He looks at his watch. It's 1.30 a.m.

Mm, he thinks, Henry hasn't woken up yet. I can't hear him. Perhaps he'll crow soon. That will be nice. Crow, Henry, crow!

15

But Angus doesn't hear Henry! He suddenly hears the two cats! He goes to the window and looks out. He can't see the cats, but he can hear them. They're crying like babies.

"Silly cats," Angus shouts.

Angus gets his torch and switches it on. He looks into the garden. The light from the torch moves slowly up and down the garden. The figure with the bag stands quietly behind a tree and doesn't move.

Suddenly, the cats cry again. Angus sees them in the torchlight. He throws a shoe at them and they run away.

"Silly cats!" he whispers and he goes back to bed.

It's quiet again in the garden.

16

"Ah!" the figure whispers and walks across the garden. But it's very dark and the figure crashes into Angus's big dustbin. The dustbin hits the ground with a loud crash. Angus jumps out of bed and runs to the window.

"Those cats!" Angus shouts. He switches on his torch and looks for his other shoe. Then he runs to the window and throws it into the garden. It hits the dustbin with a loud noise. *Crash!*

Angus goes back to bed and in a minute he is dreaming again.

The figure moves quietly out of the garden with Henry in the bag! The cats go out of the garden, too, and it is quiet again.

Part 4: Dinner for two

On Sunday morning, Maisie Plumley was working in her garden. She was happy.

Angus was in his garden, too. He was looking at the ground and he wasn't very happy.

"Good morning, Mr MacFee," Maisie called. "How are you today?"

"Not very well," Angus said. "I didn't sleep well."

"Oh, I'm sorry," Maisie said. "I slept *very* well last night."

"Didn't you hear those cats?" Angus asked.

"Cats? No, I didn't hear any cats," Maisie answered. "I slept like a baby."

"Those cats woke me up," Angus said.

Angus looked round his garden.
  "What have you lost, Mr MacFee?" Maisie asked.
  "I've lost my shoes."
  "Your shoes?"
  "I threw them at the cats!" Maisie laughed.

"Mr MacFee," she said. "I want to ask you to dinner."
  "That's very kind, Mrs Plumley. When? Next week?"
  "Well . . . tonight, at 7.30?"
  "Tonight? Well, yes, thank you."

Angus smiled. "That's nice," he said, "but I must find my shoes first. I can't come without my shoes. Ah! Here's one near the dustbin – and here's the other."
  "I'll see you tonight," Maisie said.

Maisie went into the kitchen. She was very excited. After lunch, she cooked a beautiful meal for the evening.

This will be very nice, she thought. Angus will love it. He's a very nice man, really.

20

Angus was happy, too.

Mrs Plumley is a very nice woman, he thought, and she's asked me to dinner. At five o'clock he began to dress for dinner. He dressed slowly and carefully. He put on his best suit.

Maisie's dinner was cooking and – mm! – it smelt very good.

Maisie began to dress for dinner, too. She dressed slowly and carefully. She put on her best clothes and her best shoes. Then she waited for Angus.

Angus arrived at 7.30. He had some flowers in his hand.

"They're for you," he said.

"Oh, they're beautiful. Come in. Come in, Mr MacFee."

He followed her into the house.

"Sit down, Mr MacFee."

"Thank you, Mrs Plumley."

"That's a very nice suit."

"I don't often wear my best suit these days."

"I don't often wear my best clothes," she said.

They went into the dining room. There was a big dish on the table.

"Dinner for two," she said.

"Yes, dinner for two," he said. "And it smells very good!"

"This is a delicious meal. You're a very good cook, Mrs Plumley. Really, you are."

"Thank you, Mr MacFee, but please call me 'Maisie'."

"And please call me 'Angus'."

Maisie and Angus smiled.

"Some more chicken, Angus?"

"Yes, please, Maisie. What's the name of this dish?"

"It's called 'Country chicken'."

"'Country chicken', eh? It's delicious. Really, it is."

"Yes, I like it, too. Some more bread, Angus?"

"Yes, please, Maisie. I need it for the sauce. This sauce is delicious. I like this 'Country chicken' very much."

"I'm glad," Maisie said.

Angus liked the dinner, but his eyes were sad.

"Are you all right?" Maisie asked.

"I've remembered poor Henry," Angus answered.

"Henry?" Maisie asked.

"Yes, you know, my rooster. I haven't seen him all day. He wasn't in the shed and he wasn't in the garden."

"Perhaps those cats got him," Maisie said. Her face was red and she looked at her dish.

"Perhaps," Angus said. "But I'm going to the police tomorrow."

"The police?" Maisie asked. "Oh! More chicken, Angus?"

"Yes, please," Angus said, and he gave her his plate. "With a lot of sauce, please."

23

Part 5: We can thank Henry . . .
On Monday morning, Sergeant Bloggs went to Angus's house. "Your rooster has disappeared, Mr MacFee," the sergeant said.

"Yes, sergeant. Perhaps the cats got him."

"No, I don't think so. There's blood in the shed, but there aren't many feathers. There's blood under that tree and there aren't any feathers. We can follow a line of blood across your garden," said the sergeant.

"Look, there's blood here and here . . . and look, the blood goes next door. Perhaps your new neighbour, Mrs Plumley, knows about your rooster. How did he disappear? Perhaps she knows. Perhaps she can tell us."

"Excuse me, Mrs Plumley. I'm Sergeant Bloggs. Um . . . Mr MacFee's rooster has disappeared. There's blood in his garden and your garden."

"Yes, I can explain, sergeant," Maisie said. Her face was red.

"I did it. I killed the rooster."

"Killed? You mean, *murdered*!"

"It wasn't murder, Angus. You liked the meal, didn't you?"

"You mean the 'Country chicken'?"

"Yes. The 'Country chicken' was your rooster."

"Poor Henry."

"Yes, I'm sorry, Angus." Maisie explained things to Angus and to Sergeant Bloggs. "I couldn't sleep for *weeks*!"

25

"So you killed the rooster," Sergeant Bloggs said. "I won't make trouble for you, Mrs Plumley, but you must pay for the rooster."

"Oh, yes, of course. I'll pay Angus for the rooster."

"But I don't want money. I want my Henry. I want a rooster."

"Then you must buy a rooster for Mr MacFee," Bloggs said.

"Oh, no. Not a rooster. Please. *Please*, Angus, not a rooster. I can't live next to a rooster.

"I'll buy a duck for you. A duck quacks, but it doesn't crow. I'll get you a nice duck and you can have duck eggs for breakfast. Big duck eggs."

"All right," Angus said.

"Good," said the sergeant.

26

Two weeks later, Angus had a fine duck. Her name was Henrietta. She quacked, but she didn't crow and there were a lot of big duck eggs for breakfast. Angus was happy and Maisie was happy, too.

They were good friends again.
  "It's Sunday tomorrow, Maisie," Angus said. "Come to lunch. Come at 12.30."
  "That's kind, Angus."
  "I can cook, too, you know."
  "Thank you, Angus."

Maisie slept very well that night. She dreamed of lunch with Angus. And Angus slept very well, too. He dreamed of lunch with Maisie. And the cats slept very well, too. They dreamed of lunch in the garden.

On Sunday morning, Angus was very busy. He cooked a nice meal and he smiled all morning.

I've never been so happy, he thought. Mm. This smells good. Now I can make the sauce!

Then he began to dress for lunch. He dressed slowly and carefully in his best suit.

Maisie put on her best clothes and her best shoes. Then she went next door. She had a beautiful flower in her hand.

She arrived at 12.30. "This is for you," she said, and she gave Angus a red rose. "It's from my garden."

"A red rose? For me? Oh!" Angus cried. "It's beautiful. Come in, please, Maisie."

They went into the dining room. The dish was on the table.

"Mm. It smells good. What is it?" Maisie asked.

"I can't tell you. It's a surprise," Angus answered, and they both sat down.

Then Angus showed Maisie the dish. It *was* a surprise.

"It's duck in orange sauce." Maisie cried, "It's not . . .?"

"No, it's not Henrietta!" Angus laughed.

"Mm. It's delicious."

They finished their meal. Then Angus whispered: "Maisie, I want to ask you a question. You're a widow and I'm a widower. We live alone. . ."

"Yes, Angus!" Maisie cried. "We can thank Henry for this!"

29

On Monday morning, Hawkins' General Store was full of people.

"Have you heard the news?" Mrs Carpe cried.

"News? What news?" the women in the shop cried. "Tell us. Tell us. Quickly!"

"There will be a wedding in Puddleton soon."

"A wedding? Who . . .?"

"Angus and Maisie!" And Mrs Carpe told them the story. She told them about Henry and the 'Country chicken' and the duck.

"Hm," Mrs Nosey said. "I knew all that from the start."

"Well, they can thank Henry for this," Mrs Carpe cried. *"Cock-a-doodle-doo!"*

"Cock-a-doodle-doo!" they answered in a loud voice.

Questions

Read pages 2 to 4. Then answer these questions.
  Where is Hawkins' General Store?
  Who was Angus MacFee's new neighbour?
  Why was Mrs Carpe excited? (*Answer*: Because . . .)
  What does Maisie have to do in her garden?

After page 8, answer these questions.
  Where did Maisie Plumley see Angus MacFee?
  Who was a widow, and who was a widower?
  Why did Maisie look at her watch? (*Answer*:
    Because . . .)
  What does Henry never know?

After page 12:
  Where did the women talk about Maisie?
  Who said, "We must help Maisie Plumley"?
  Why was Maisie always tired?
  What is Angus doing at 1 a.m. on Saturday night?

After page 16:
  Where can you see an axe?
  Who shouts at the cats?
  Why will Henry never crow again?
  What does Angus throw at the cats?

After page 20:
  Where were Angus's shoes?
  Who asked Angus to dinner?

  Why were Angus's shoes not in the house?
  What did Angus and Maisie wear for dinner?

After page 24:
  Where was the big dish?
  Who made the "Country chicken"?
  Why were Angus's eyes sad?
  What did Angus do on Monday morning?

After page 28:
  Where did Sergeant Bloggs see blood?
  Who was the "figure" in Henry's garden?
  Why did Maisie kill Henry?
  What did Maisie take to Angus's house?

After page 30:
  Who took the news to Hawkins' General Store?
  Why was Mrs Carpe excited?
  What noise did the people in Hawkins' General
    Store make?

Did you understand the story?
  Angus MacFee was a ___ . His new ___ was Maisie
  Plumley, and she was a ___ . Angus's ___ crowed
  all night, and Maisie couldn't ___ . She put it in a
  delicious "Country ___" dish and Angus liked it.
  Maisie bought a ___ for Angus. He asked Maisie to
  ___ . They had ___ in ___ sauce, but it wasn't
  ___ . In the end, there was a wedding in the village
  of ___ .

31

LONGMAN GROUP UK LIMITED
Longman House, Burnt Mill, Harlow,
Essex, CM20 2JE England
and Associated Companies throughout the world.

First published 1983
Fourth impression 1987

Produced by Longman Group (FE) Ltd
Printed in Hong Kong

ISBN 0-582-54081-X